Google Workspace

FOR BEGINNERS

The Complete Step-By-Step Handbook Guide To Learning And Mastering All Of Google's Collaborative Apps (Gmail, Drive, Sheets, Docs, Slides, Forms, Etc)

GOOGLE WORKSPACE FOR BEGINNERS

The Complete Step-By-Step Handbook Guide To Learning And Mastering All Of Google's Collaborative Apps (Gmail, Drive, Sheets, Docs, Slides, Forms, Etc)

GOOGLE WORKSPACE FOR BEGINNERS: THE COMPLETE STEP-BY-STEP HANDBOOK GUIDE TO LEARNING AND MASTERING ALL OF GOOGLE'S COLLABORATIVE APPS (GMAIL, DRIVE, SHEETS, DOCS, SLIDES, FORMS, ETC)

First edition. November 28, 2023.

Written by Voltaire Lumiere.

TABLE OF CONTENTS

CHAPTER 1
GETTING STARTED WITH GOOGLE WORKSPACE

- **Understanding the Ecosystem**

In the ever-evolving landscape of digital collaboration, Google Workspace stands as a comprehensive ecosystem designed to streamline communication and productivity. Comprising an array of interconnected applications, this suite caters to diverse needs within professional settings. At its core, Google Workspace is more than a collection of tools; it's a dynamic platform transforming the way individuals and teams interact in the virtual realm.

At the heart of Google Workspace lies a robust set of collaborative applications, including Gmail, Google Drive, Calendar, and more. Each component seamlessly integrates, fostering a unified environment where users can fluidly navigate between tasks, communications, and data management.

Gmail, the cornerstone of this ecosystem, transcends conventional email platforms. Beyond its fundamental function, Gmail offers an array of organizational features, allowing users to categorize, prioritize, and manage their inbox with unparalleled efficiency. Meanwhile, Google Drive serves as a centralized hub for document creation and storage. Its cloud-based architecture ensures accessibility from any device, fostering collaborative efforts in real-time.

Google Calendar, another pivotal component, redefines scheduling and time management. It not only facilitates personal organization but also supports team coordination through shared calendars and event scheduling. This interconnectedness extends to Google Meet, seamlessly integrated for virtual meetings, enhancing the fluidity of communication within the workspace.

To grasp the essence of Google Workspace is to recognize its interconnected nature—the synergy between applications, the ease of collaboration, and the intuitive design facilitating a seamless user experience. As users embark on their journey within this ecosystem, they are stepping into a realm where digital collaboration is not merely a task but an immersive and transformative experience.

- **Setting Up Your Account**

Setting up your Google Workspace account is the foundational step towards unlocking a world of collaborative possibilities. The process is straightforward, designed to ensure a secure and personalized experience tailored to your professional needs.

Begin by visiting the Google Workspace sign-up page, where you will be prompted to create a Google Account if you don't have one already. This account will serve as your gateway to the entire suite of Google Workspace applications.

During the setup, you'll be required to provide essential information, including your name, desired email address, and a secure password. This initial account creation lays the groundwork for your personalized workspace, setting the stage for efficient and secure collaboration.

Once your account is established, you gain access to the Google Workspace dashboard. Here, you'll encounter a user-friendly interface, designed for easy navigation. The dashboard serves as the command center for your digital workspace, providing quick access to Gmail, Drive, Calendar, and other integrated applications.

As part of the setup process, consider customizing your profile to enhance personalization and identity within the workspace. Upload a profile picture, update contact information, and explore additional settings to tailor your experience.

Security is paramount, and Google Workspace recognizes this by offering robust account protection features. Implement two-factor authentication for an added layer of security, ensuring the integrity of your workspace and data.

In essence, setting up your Google Workspace account is not just a technicality; it's the initiation into a collaborative ecosystem that adapts to your workflow. From this point forward, your digital workspace is ready to evolve and grow alongside your professional journey.

- **Customizing Workspace Settings**

Customizing your Google Workspace settings empowers you to tailor the digital environment to suit your specific preferences and optimize your workflow. This personalized touch ensures that your workspace is not only efficient but also reflective of your unique needs.

Navigate to the settings menu within your Google Workspace dashboard to embark on the customization journey. Here, you'll encounter a range of options that allow you to fine-tune your experience.

1. **Profile Personalization:**

- Upload a professional profile picture to personalize your account.
- Add a signature to your emails for a polished and consistent communication style.
- Set your time zone to ensure accurate scheduling in applications like Google Calendar.

2. **Theme and Display Options:**

- Explore different theme options to give your workspace a visual appeal that resonates with you.

- Adjust display density settings for applications like Gmail to optimize screen real estate based on your preferences.

3. **Language and Region Preferences:**

- Customize the language settings to work in your preferred language.
- Set your region to ensure accurate date and time formats, aligning with your local conventions.

4. **Notification Settings:**

- Tailor notification preferences to manage alerts from various applications.
- Choose how you receive notifications—via email, desktop, or mobile—to stay informed without feeling overwhelmed.

5. **Accessibility Features:**

- Explore accessibility settings to ensure an inclusive digital experience.
- Adjust font sizes, contrast, and keyboard shortcuts to accommodate individual needs.

Customizing your workspace settings is not just about aesthetics; it's about creating an environment that enhances your productivity and comfort. As you delve into the customization options, you're sculpting a workspace uniquely attuned to your work style, making your digital journey with Google Workspace a seamless and personalized experience.

- **Exploring the Workspace Interface**

1. **Dashboard Overview:**

- The dashboard is your central hub, providing a bird's-eye view of all Google Workspace applications.
- Easily switch between Gmail, Drive, Calendar, and other integrated tools directly from the dashboard.

2. **Application Menus:**

- Each application within the workspace has its dedicated menu, accessible from the top-left corner.
- Explore the menu options to access specific features, settings, and tools tailored to each application.

3. **Search Functionality:**

- The search bar, prominently positioned, facilitates swift navigation across your entire workspace.
- Use it to locate emails, documents, or events, saving valuable time in the process.

4. **Unified Navigation Bar:**

- The top navigation bar provides a unified experience, allowing seamless transitions between applications.

- Access notifications, settings, and your account profile from this centralized location.

5. **Intuitive Toolbars:**

- Within each application, intuitive toolbars offer quick access to essential functions.
- Familiarize yourself with these toolbars to streamline tasks such as composing emails, creating documents, or managing files.

As you explore the workspace interface, you'll discover a harmonious integration of design elements aimed at promoting a fluid and intuitive user experience. Whether you're drafting an email in Gmail, collaborating on a document in Drive, or scheduling an event in Calendar, the interface adapts to your needs, fostering a cohesive and user-friendly environment. This thoughtful design ensures that every interaction within the workspace is not just functional but also a step towards enhancing your overall digital experience.

- **Accessing Help and Support**

Accessing help and support within Google Workspace is a valuable resource that ensures a smooth and efficient user experience. Google recognizes the importance of providing assistance when needed, and accessing help and support is designed to be accessible and user-friendly.

1. **Google Workspace Help Center:**

- The Help Center is a comprehensive repository of articles, guides, and tutorials covering all aspects of Google Workspace.
- Accessible from the dashboard, it serves as a go-to resource for troubleshooting, learning new features, and finding answers to common queries.

2. **Contextual Help within Applications:**

- Many applications within the workspace, such as Gmail and Google Docs, offer contextual help.
- Look for the question mark icon or "Help" option within an application to access tooltips, guided tours, and specific help content relevant to the task at hand.

3. **Community Forums:**

- Google Workspace boasts a vibrant community of users who actively share insights and solutions.
- Engage with the community forums to seek advice, share experiences, and learn from the collective knowledge of other Google Workspace users.

4. **Live Chat and Email Support:**

- For personalized assistance, Google Workspace provides live chat and email support options.

- Reach out to Google's support team directly from the Help Center or your dashboard for real-time assistance with more complex issues.

5. **Training Resources and Webinars:**

- Google frequently conducts webinars and training sessions to keep users abreast of new features and best practices.
- Explore training resources, attend webinars, and participate in virtual events to deepen your understanding and proficiency in using Google Workspace.

Navigating the help and support options within Google Workspace ensures that users can seek guidance at various levels, from self-help resources to direct assistance. This commitment to user support underscores Google's dedication to empowering users to make the most of the collaborative tools at their disposal.

CHAPTER 2
MASTERING GMAIL

- **Email Basics and Management**

Email serves as the linchpin of digital communication within Google Workspace, and understanding its basics and management principles is fundamental to efficient and organized workflow.

1. **Composing and Sending Emails:**

- Initiate the email creation process by clicking on the "Compose" button.
- Craft professional emails using the rich text editor, incorporating formatting, attachments, and inline images.
- Leverage the "Send" button to dispatch your emails to recipients.

2. **Managing Your Inbox Effectively:**

- Familiarize yourself with Gmail's tabbed inbox system for categorizing emails into Primary, Social, Promotions, and other tabs.
- Utilize the priority inbox feature to automatically sort important emails to the top.

- Implement labels and filters to categorize and organize incoming emails, streamlining your inbox.

3. **Organizing Emails with Labels and Filters:**

- Labels function as virtual folders, providing a flexible way to categorize and sort emails.
- Filters automate email organization by allowing you to set rules for the automatic application of labels, marking as important, or archiving emails.

4. **Using Priority Inbox:**

- Enable Priority Inbox to automatically categorize emails based on their importance.
- Customize settings to prioritize specific senders or types of emails, ensuring that critical messages are promptly highlighted.

5. **Leveraging Snooze and Archive Functions:**

- Snooze emails to temporarily remove them from your inbox and have them resurface at a more convenient time.
- Archive emails to declutter your inbox without deleting them; archived emails are easily retrievable through search.

Mastering email basics and management in Google Workspace goes beyond sending and receiving messages; it's about adopting a systematic approach to organization and prioritization, optimizing your communication workflow for enhanced productivity.

- **Organizing with Labels and Filters**

Effectively organizing your Gmail inbox involves harnessing the power of labels and filters, two robust features that bring order and efficiency to your email management.

1. **Creating and Applying Labels:**

- Labels are virtual tags that you can assign to emails for easy categorization.
- Create custom labels based on projects, clients, or specific topics by navigating to the "Labels" section in settings.
- Apply labels to emails manually or automate the process using filters for seamless organization.

2. **Setting Up Filters for Automated Organization:**

- Filters are rules that automatically perform actions on incoming emails based on specified criteria.
- Access the "Filters and Blocked Addresses" section in settings to create custom filters.
- Define filter criteria such as sender, subject, or keywords, and choose actions like applying labels, archiving, or categorizing.

3. **Customizing Label Colors and Visibility:**

- Personalize your labels by assigning distinct colors for quick visual identification.
- Adjust label visibility in the left sidebar to prioritize frequently used labels, ensuring easy access.

4. **Creating Nested Labels for Hierarchical Organization:**

- Establish a hierarchy by creating nested labels within broader categories.
- This tiered approach aids in organizing complex projects or varied aspects of your professional life.

5. **Managing and Editing Labels:**

- Regularly review and edit labels to adapt to evolving organizational needs.
- Merge similar labels, update colors, or refine criteria for automated filtering to maintain an efficient labeling system.

Harnessing labels and filters within Gmail transforms your inbox into a finely tuned organizational tool. By strategically applying labels and automating actions with filters, you not only streamline your email management but also ensure that relevant messages are readily accessible, allowing you to focus on what matters most in your workflow.

- **Productivity Features in Gmail**

Gmail offers a suite of productivity features that extend beyond conventional email functionalities, empowering users to manage their communications with efficiency and ease.

1. **Using Priority Inbox:**

- Priority Inbox intelligently categorizes emails based on their importance and your interaction history.
- Train Priority Inbox by marking emails as important or unimportant to enhance its accuracy over time.
- Quickly access crucial emails at the top of your inbox, streamlining your response workflow.

2. **Snooze and Schedule Emails:**

- Snooze emails to temporarily remove them from your inbox and have them reappear at a later, more convenient time.
- Schedule emails to be sent at a specific date and time, ensuring timely delivery without the need for manual follow-up.

3. **Smart Compose for Quick Email Composition:**

- Smart Compose suggests completions to your sentences as you type, accelerating the email composition process.

- Embrace predictive text suggestions that adapt to your writing style over time, saving keystrokes and boosting overall writing efficiency.

4. **Mute and Unsubscribe for Noise Reduction:**

- Mute email threads to prevent unnecessary notifications from continuous replies in group conversations.
- Utilize the "Unsubscribe" feature for newsletters and promotional emails, decluttering your inbox from unwanted subscriptions.

5. **Customizing Keyboard Shortcuts:**

- Enable and customize keyboard shortcuts to navigate Gmail effortlessly.
- Speed up your workflow by using shortcuts for tasks like composing, archiving, and navigating between emails without relying on the mouse.

By integrating these productivity features into your Gmail experience, you transform your email platform into a dynamic tool that adapts to your workflow. These functionalities not only save time but also enhance your overall email management, allowing you to focus on the core tasks that drive your productivity.

- **Collaboration Tools in Gmail**

Gmail is not just an email platform; it's a hub for collaboration, offering tools that facilitate seamless communication and teamwork directly within your inbox.

1. **Sharing Emails and Attachments:**

- Collaborate effortlessly by sharing entire email threads or specific messages with colleagues.
- Attachments can be shared directly from Google Drive, ensuring version control and access to the latest documents.

2. **Google Meet Integration:**

- Initiate video meetings directly from Gmail with Google Meet integration.
- Schedule, join, or start impromptu meetings without leaving your inbox, enhancing real-time collaboration.

3. **Chat in Gmail:**

- Google Chat is seamlessly integrated into Gmail, providing a dynamic chat platform.
- Engage in one-on-one or group chats, share files, and collaborate in real time without switching between applications.

4. **Assigning Tasks with Google Tasks:**

- Google Tasks allows you to create and manage to-do lists directly within Gmail.
- Convert emails into tasks, set due dates, and collaborate with team members on shared task lists for streamlined project management.

5. **Real-time Editing with Google Docs Attachments:**

- Attach Google Docs files directly to emails for collaborative editing.
- Multiple users can simultaneously work on the document, fostering real-time collaboration without the need for constant file attachments.

By integrating these collaboration tools into Gmail, users can transcend traditional email boundaries and transform their inbox into a dynamic workspace. Whether it's scheduling virtual meetings, collaborating on documents, or managing tasks, Gmail serves as a central hub for streamlined teamwork and enhanced productivity.

- **Advanced Tips and Tricks**

Unlock the full potential of Gmail with advanced tips and tricks that go beyond the basics, allowing you to navigate and optimize your email experience with finesse.

1. **Mastering Keyboard Shortcuts:**

- Accelerate your workflow by mastering Gmail's extensive set of keyboard shortcuts.
- Navigate, compose, and manage emails with efficiency using key combinations, saving valuable time.

2. **Utilizing Advanced Search Operators:**

- Refine your search queries using advanced search operators to pinpoint specific emails.
- Combine operators such as "from," "subject," and "label" for precise and rapid search results.

3. **Creating Custom Filters:**

- Dive deeper into email automation by creating custom filters based on complex criteria.
- Specify multiple conditions for filtering, archiving, labeling, or forwarding emails automatically.

4. **Personalizing Your Inbox with Multiple Inboxes:**

- Enhance your inbox organization by enabling multiple inboxes.
- Create customized sections within your inbox to display specific labels, starred emails, or other criteria for a tailored view.

5. **Enabling Offline Mode:**

- Stay productive even without an internet connection by enabling Gmail's offline mode.
- Access and respond to emails, and compose drafts offline, with changes syncing once you're back online.

6. **Undo Send Feature:**

- Activate the "Undo Send" feature to give yourself a brief window to retract sent emails.
- Set the time delay for message retrieval in the settings to prevent accidental sends.

7. **Customizing Swipe Actions on Mobile:**

- Tailor swipe actions on the Gmail mobile app for quick and personalized email management.
- Choose actions such as archiving, deleting, marking as read, or moving emails with a simple swipe gesture.

By incorporating these advanced tips and tricks into your Gmail routine, you elevate your email proficiency, gaining control over intricate features and enhancing your overall user experience. These strategies empower you to navigate Gmail with finesse, ensuring that you harness its full capabilities for efficient communication and productivity.

CHAPTER 3

MASTERING GOOGLE DRIVE

- **Google Drive Basics**

1. **Uploading and Organizing Files:**

- Upload files and folders to Google Drive by dragging and dropping or using the "New" button.
- Organize content with the intuitive folder structure, creating a hierarchy that suits your needs.

2. **Navigating Folders and File Management:**

- Navigate through folders to locate files easily.
- Utilize file management options such as renaming, moving, and deleting to maintain a tidy and efficient file structure.

3. **Collaborative Document Creation with Google Docs:**

- Create documents directly within Google Drive using Google Docs.
- Collaborate in real-time with others, making edits, leaving comments, and tracking changes seamlessly.

4. **Creating and Organizing Spreadsheets in Google Sheets:**

- Develop spreadsheets using Google Sheets for data analysis and collaboration.

- Leverage functions and formulas to perform calculations, and share the sheet with others for collaborative editing.

5. **Designing Presentations with Google Slides:**

- Craft visually appealing presentations in Google Slides.

- Collaborate on slideshows in real time, incorporating multimedia elements and animations for engaging presentations.

6. **Storing and Analyzing Data with Google Forms:**

- Collect and analyze data efficiently by creating custom forms in Google Forms.

- Link form responses directly to Google Sheets for seamless data management and analysis.

7. **Real-time Collaboration Features:**

- Leverage real-time collaboration features across all Google Drive applications.

- Multiple users can work simultaneously on documents, spreadsheets, and presentations, fostering efficient teamwork.

Understanding these Google Drive basics lays the foundation for harnessing the platform's collaborative power. Whether you're working on individual projects or engaging in team collaborations,

Google Drive provides a centralized and accessible space for efficient file management and seamless document creation.

- **Collaborative Document Creation**

Collaborative document creation in Google Drive, particularly with Google Docs, offers a dynamic and real-time approach to teamwork. Here's an exploration of the key aspects of creating documents collaboratively:

1. **Creating a New Document:**

- Begin by clicking on "New" in Google Drive and selecting "Google Docs."

- Alternatively, within Google Docs, choose "File" and then "New Document."

2. **Real-time Editing and Collaboration:**

- Invite collaborators by clicking the "Share" button in the top-right corner.

- Collaborators can simultaneously edit the document, with changes reflected in real-time.

3. **Commenting and Suggestions:**

- Enhance communication by using the commenting feature to discuss specific parts of the document.

- Make suggestions that collaborators can accept or reject, providing a structured approach to edits.

4. **Version History and Revision Tracking:**

- Access the document's version history under "File" to view changes over time.
- Revert to previous versions or review edits made by collaborators, maintaining a comprehensive record.

5. **Offline Editing:**

- Enable offline mode to continue editing documents without an internet connection.
- Changes made offline will sync once a connection is reestablished.

6. **Inserting Media and Links:**

- Enhance the document by inserting images, charts, and links.
- Collaborators can see these additions in real-time, fostering a visually rich and interactive document.

7. **Formatting and Styles:**

- Use the formatting options to structure the document with headings, bullet points, and numbered lists.

- Collaborators can maintain consistent styles, ensuring a polished and professional appearance.

8. **Exporting and Sharing:**

- Collaborators can export the document in various formats, such as PDF or Microsoft Word.
- Share the finalized document with a broader audience or specific stakeholders.

By embracing collaborative document creation in Google Docs, teams can efficiently work together, fostering creativity, communication, and productivity. The platform's real-time editing, commenting, and version control features ensure a seamless collaborative experience, making it an invaluable tool for projects, reports, and any other document-centric tasks.

- **Spreadsheets in Google Sheets**

Google Sheets provides a powerful and collaborative environment for creating and managing spreadsheets. Here's a look at the essentials of working with spreadsheets in Google Sheets:

1. **Creating a New Spreadsheet:**

- Start a new spreadsheet by clicking on "New" in Google Drive and selecting "Google Sheets."
- Alternatively, within Google Sheets, choose "File" and then "New Spreadsheet."

2. **Navigating the Spreadsheet Interface:**

- Familiarize yourself with the cells, rows, and columns that make up the spreadsheet grid.
- Use the tabs at the bottom to navigate between different sheets within a spreadsheet.

3. **Entering Data and Formulas:**

- Enter data into cells by simply clicking and typing.
- Use formulas and functions to perform calculations. Begin a formula with the "=" sign, and explore functions like SUM, AVERAGE, and VLOOKUP for advanced calculations.

4. **Formatting and Styling:**

- Format cells to change text alignment, font, and background color.
- Apply cell borders and styles to enhance the visual appeal of your spreadsheet.

5. **Data Sorting and Filtering:**

- Easily sort data in ascending or descending order.
- Use the filter tool to display specific subsets of data based on custom criteria.

6. **Collaborative Editing:**

- Share your spreadsheet with collaborators by clicking the "Share" button.
- Collaborators can simultaneously edit the spreadsheet, and changes are reflected in real-time.

7. **Charts and Graphs:**

- Visualize data with a variety of chart options.
- Insert charts directly into the spreadsheet, and they will dynamically update as data changes.

8. **Data Validation and Protection:**

- Apply data validation to control the type of data entered into a cell.
- Protect sheets and ranges to control access and prevent accidental edits.

9. **Importing and Exporting Data:**

- Import data from external sources or export your spreadsheet in various formats, including PDF and Microsoft Excel.

10. **Version History and Collaboration Features:**

- Track changes using the version history feature under "File."

- Collaborators can leave comments and suggestions, enhancing communication during collaborative projects.

Google Sheets provides a collaborative and dynamic platform for data management and analysis. Whether you're handling budgets, creating project timelines, or conducting data analysis, the features within Google Sheets empower users to work efficiently and collaboratively on spreadsheet-based tasks.

- **Designing Presentations with Google Slides**

Google Slides is a versatile tool for creating visually appealing and collaborative presentations. Here's a guide to designing presentations effectively with Google Slides:

1. **Creating a New Presentation:**

- Begin by selecting "Google Slides" from the "New" menu in Google Drive.
- Alternatively, within Google Slides, choose "File" and then "New Presentation."

2. **Choosing a Theme:**

- Explore a range of themes available in Google Slides.
- Select a theme that complements your presentation's content and style.

3. **Adding Slides and Content:**

- Use the toolbar to add new slides with different layouts, such as title slides, content slides, and more.
- Insert text, images, and shapes into slides to convey your message effectively.

4. **Formatting and Styling:**

- Customize the appearance of text and shapes using the formatting options.
- Apply consistent styling, such as font choices and color schemes, for a polished and professional look.

5. **Inserting Images and Media:**

- Enhance your presentation by inserting images, graphics, and multimedia.
- Use the "Insert" menu to add images directly from Google Drive or the web.

6. **Working with Transitions and Animations:**

- Create engaging presentations by adding transitions between slides.
- Apply animations to individual elements for a dynamic and interactive experience.

7. **Collaborative Editing and Commenting:**

- Share your presentation with collaborators by clicking the "Share" button.
- Collaborators can edit the presentation in real-time and leave comments for feedback and suggestions.

8. **Embedding Charts and Diagrams:**

- Utilize the power of Google Sheets integration to embed live charts and diagrams.
- Any changes made to the linked spreadsheet will automatically update in the presentation.

9. **Presenting and Speaker Notes:**

- Rehearse and present directly from Google Slides using the "Present" button.
- Add speaker notes to provide additional information or cues during the presentation.

10. **Sharing and Exporting:**

- Share your presentation with others by generating a shareable link or inviting specific collaborators.
- Export the presentation in various formats, including PDF and Microsoft PowerPoint.

By leveraging these features, Google Slides becomes a dynamic canvas for creating visually stunning presentations. Its collaborative nature and integration with other Google Workspace applications make it a powerful tool for team projects, lectures, and business presentations.

- **Storing and Analyzing Data with Google Forms**

Google Forms is a versatile tool that simplifies the process of collecting and analyzing data through custom surveys, quizzes, and forms. Here's a guide to storing and analyzing data effectively with Google Forms:

1. **Creating a New Form:**

- Start a new form by selecting "Google Forms" from the "New" menu in Google Drive.
- Alternatively, within Google Forms, click on the "+" button to create a new form.

2. **Designing Form Questions:**

- Add various question types, such as multiple-choice, short answer, or scale, to gather specific types of information.
- Customize the look of your form by changing themes and backgrounds.

3. **Utilizing Form Logic:**

- Implement conditional logic to show or hide specific questions based on respondents' previous answers.
- Create a personalized and dynamic experience for respondents.

4. **Embedding Media and Additional Content:**

- Enhance your forms by embedding images, videos, or informative text.
- Use multimedia elements to provide context or clarification for questions.

5. **Collecting Responses:**

- Share your form by sending a direct link, embedding it on a website, or distributing it through email or social media.
- Track responses in real-time through the "Responses" tab in Google Forms.

6. **Data Validation and Required Questions:**

- Apply data validation rules to ensure that respondents enter accurate information.
- Make certain questions mandatory by marking them as required.

7. **Viewing and Analyzing Responses:**

- Access response data in real-time within Google Forms or export it to Google Sheets for further analysis.
- Explore response summaries and visualizations provided by Google Forms for quick insights.

8. **Integrating with Google Sheets:**

- Connect your form to a Google Sheets spreadsheet to store and manage responses.
- Automatically update the linked spreadsheet as new responses are submitted.

9. **Setting up Notifications:**

- Receive email notifications for new responses by configuring form settings.
- Stay informed and respond promptly to incoming data.

10. **Sharing Collaborative Forms:**

- Collaborate with others by inviting them to edit the form collaboratively.
- Foster teamwork in creating and refining data collection instruments.

Google Forms simplifies the entire process of data collection and analysis, offering a user-friendly platform for creating customized forms and surveys. Whether it's for academic research, customer feedback, or event planning, Google Forms streamlines data gathering and provides valuable insights for informed decision-making.

CHAPTER 4

COLLABORATIVE WORK IN GOOGLE WORKSPACE

- **Real-time Collaboration Features**

Real-time collaboration is a hallmark of Google Workspace, enabling users to work seamlessly with others on documents, spreadsheets, and presentations. Here's an overview of the key real-time collaboration features:

1. **Simultaneous Editing:**

- Multiple users can edit a document, spreadsheet, or presentation simultaneously.
- Changes made by one user are instantly visible to others, fostering real-time collaboration.

2. **Comments and Suggestions:**

- Collaborators can leave comments on specific sections of a document, spreadsheet, or presentation.
- Suggestions mode allows users to propose edits that can be accepted or rejected by the document owner.

3. **Real-time Cursor Presence:**

- See the cursor positions of collaborators in real-time.

- Each user's cursor is color-coded, making it easy to identify who is editing or reviewing.

4. **Version History:**

- Access the version history to review changes made over time.
- Users can revert to previous versions or identify contributors to specific edits.

5. **Chat and Communication:**

- Integrated chat features in documents and presentations allow collaborators to communicate directly.
- Streamline discussions without leaving the document interface.

6. **Presence Indicators:**

- Presence indicators show when collaborators are actively viewing or editing the document.
- Green indicates active participation, enhancing real-time awareness.

7. **Real-time Collaboration in Google Forms:**

- Multiple users can collaborate on the creation and editing of Google Forms.

- Changes are reflected instantly, ensuring a cohesive and collaborative form-building process.

8. **Collaboration in Google Drawings:**

- Google Drawings support real-time collaboration, allowing multiple users to create and edit drawings simultaneously.
- Collaborators can insert shapes, lines, and text in real-time.

9. **Access Control and Permissions:**

- Set specific permissions for collaborators, such as editing, commenting, or viewing only.
- Maintain control over who can access and modify the document.

10. **Integration with Google Chat and Meet:**

- Seamlessly transition from document collaboration to real-time communication using Google Chat.
- Initiate Google Meet sessions directly from the document interface for face-to-face collaboration.

These real-time collaboration features redefine how teams work together, breaking down geographical barriers and fostering dynamic interaction. Whether in a document, spreadsheet, presentation, or other collaborative workspace, Google Workspace's robust set of features ensures a fluid and efficient collaborative experience.

- **Sharing and Permissions**

Sharing and permissions in Google Workspace are crucial aspects that allow you to control access to your documents, spreadsheets, presentations, and other files. Here's a comprehensive guide on sharing and setting permissions:

1. **Sharing a File:**

- Click on the "Share" button located in the top-right corner of your document, spreadsheet, or presentation.
- Alternatively, you can click on the "Share" option in the file menu.

2. **Choosing Visibility Options:**

- Decide on the visibility of your file: public on the web, anyone with the link, or restricted to specific people or groups.

3. **Setting Permissions:**

- Choose who can access your file and the level of access they have.
- Permission options include:
    - **Viewer:** Can view the file but not make edits.

- **Commenter:** Can view and leave comments but not make edits.
- **Editor:** Can view, comment, and make edits.

4. **Sharing with Specific People:**

- Enter the email addresses of individuals or groups you want to share the file with.
- Set permissions for each person or group individually.

5. **Sharing Links:**

- Generate a shareable link with specific permissions.
- Share the link with anyone, granting them access according to the specified permissions.

6. **Notification Options:**

- Choose whether to send email notifications to collaborators when sharing the file.
- Notify collaborators when you make changes or add comments.

7. **Advanced Sharing Settings:**

- Access advanced settings to control options like preventing viewers from downloading, copying, or printing the file.

- Restrict access to specific domains for enhanced security.

8. **Changing Permissions:**

- You can change permissions at any time by revisiting the "Share" settings.
- Remove or add collaborators, adjust their permissions, or change visibility options as needed.

9. **Shared Drives (Formerly Team Drives):**

- For collaborative work within a team, consider using Shared Drives.
- Shared Drives provide a space where files are owned by the team, not an individual, ensuring continuity even if team members change.

10. **Accessing Shared Files:**

- Collaborators can access shared files directly from their Google Drive or via the shared link.
- Shared files appear in the "Shared with Me" section of Google Drive.

By mastering sharing and permissions in Google Workspace, you gain control over who can access, edit, and collaborate on your files, ensuring a secure and collaborative digital workspace. These features are pivotal in facilitating efficient collaboration while maintaining data privacy and security.

- **Version History and Revision Tracking**

Version history and revision tracking in Google Workspace provide valuable tools for tracking changes made to documents, spreadsheets, and presentations. Here's a guide on utilizing these features:

1. **Accessing Version History:**

- In a document, spreadsheet, or presentation, click on "File" in the top-left corner.
- Select "Version history" and then "See version history."

2. **Viewing Changes Over Time:**

- The version history panel will display a timeline of changes made to the document.
- Each version is time-stamped, allowing you to track the evolution of the file.

3. **Previewing Versions:**

- Click on a specific version to preview the document as it appeared at that point in time.

- This is especially useful for reviewing changes made by collaborators.

4. **Restoring Previous Versions:**

- To revert to a previous version, select the version you want to restore.
- Click on "Restore this version" to replace the current version with the selected one.

5. **Naming Versions:**

- Give important versions custom names for easy identification.
- This is particularly useful when collaborating on projects with multiple iterations.

6. **Revision History in Google Docs:**

- In Google Docs, you can access a detailed revision history by clicking on the "All changes saved in Drive" link at the top-right corner.
- This provides a comprehensive view of changes made by different collaborators.

7. **Cell and Sheet History in Google Sheets:**

- In Google Sheets, you can view the revision history for specific cells or sheets.

- Right-click on a cell, range, or sheet tab and select "Show edit history" to see who made changes and when.

8. **Presentation Slide Revisions:**

- In Google Slides, view the revision history by clicking on "File" and then "See revision history."

- Explore changes made to individual slides and revert to specific versions.

9. **Collaborator Colors:**

- Each collaborator's changes are highlighted in a specific color.

- This visual representation aids in identifying who made specific edits.

10. **Integration with Google Drive:**

- The version history is seamlessly integrated with Google Drive.

- Even if you're not actively viewing the version history, changes are automatically saved and can be accessed later.

Version history and revision tracking empower users to monitor and manage changes effectively, ensuring a transparent and collaborative editing process. These features are particularly valuable in group projects where multiple contributors may be working on the same document, spreadsheet, or presentation simultaneously.

- **Google Workspace Integration**

Google Workspace Integration is a key feature that allows seamless collaboration across various applications within the Google ecosystem. Here's an overview of how Google Workspace applications are integrated:

1. **Unified User Account:**

- A single Google account provides access to the entire suite of Google Workspace applications.

- Users can seamlessly switch between Gmail, Google Drive, Google Docs, Sheets, Slides, and other tools using the same login credentials.

2. **Real-time Collaboration:**

- Google Workspace applications are designed for real-time collaboration.

- Multiple users can work simultaneously on documents, spreadsheets, and presentations, with changes visible in real-time.

3. **File Integration Across Applications:**

- Files created in one Google Workspace app can be easily integrated into others.

- For example, a Google Doc can be linked directly in a Gmail email or embedded in a Google Slides presentation.

4. **Calendar Integration:**

- Google Calendar is seamlessly integrated with Gmail.
- Calendar events, invitations, and schedules are accessible directly from the Gmail interface.

5. **Google Meet Integration:**

- Google Meet is integrated into various Google Workspace applications.
- Users can initiate video meetings directly from Gmail, Google Calendar, or Google Docs for enhanced collaboration.

6. **Shared Drive (Formerly Team Drive) Integration:**

- Shared Drives provide a collaborative space where files are owned by a team, not an individual.
- Files in Shared Drives are seamlessly integrated with Google Docs, Sheets, and Slides.

7. **Google Chat Integration:**

- Google Chat is integrated into Gmail, offering a streamlined communication platform.

- Users can engage in real-time chat conversations while working on documents or collaborating in other applications.

8. **Google Forms Integration:**

- Google Forms can be seamlessly integrated into Google Sheets.
- Form responses are automatically collected and organized in a linked Google Sheet for efficient data management.

9. **Google Keep Integration:**

- Google Keep, a note-taking app, is integrated with other Google Workspace applications.
- Users can access their notes and ideas directly from Gmail or Google Docs.

10. **Cross-Application Search:**

- The search functionality is integrated across Google Workspace applications.
- Users can search for emails, documents, and other files from a central search bar in Gmail or Google Drive.

The tight integration of Google Workspace applications streamlines workflows, enhances productivity, and fosters a cohesive digital workspace. Whether it's collaborating on documents, scheduling meetings, or communicating with team members, the seamless integration ensures a unified and efficient user experience.

- **Best Practices for Team Productivity**

Optimizing team productivity is crucial for achieving success in any organization. Here are some best practices for enhancing team productivity:

1. **Define Clear Goals:**

- Establish clear and measurable goals for the team.
- Ensure that every team member understands the overarching objectives and their individual roles in achieving them.

2. **Effective Communication:**

- Foster open and transparent communication channels.
- Utilize collaboration tools such as Slack, Microsoft Teams, or Google Chat to facilitate real-time communication and document sharing.

3. **Utilize Project Management Tools:**

- Implement project management tools like Asana, Trello, or Jira to organize tasks, set deadlines, and track progress.
- These tools help teams stay organized and on top of their work.

4. **Encourage Collaboration:**

- Foster a collaborative environment where team members can share ideas and insights.
- Use collaborative platforms like Google Workspace or Microsoft 365 to enable real-time editing and feedback on documents.

5. **Set Realistic Deadlines:**

- Establish realistic timelines for projects and tasks.
- Avoid overloading team members with unrealistic expectations, as this can lead to burnout and decreased productivity.

6. **Provide Adequate Training:**

- Ensure that team members are proficient in the tools and technologies they use.
- Provide training sessions and resources to help team members maximize their efficiency.

7. **Flexibility and Work-Life Balance:**

- Encourage a healthy work-life balance to prevent burnout.
- Be flexible with work hours when possible, and promote a culture that values well-being.

8. **Recognize and Reward Achievements:**

- Acknowledge and celebrate team achievements, both big and small.
- Recognition boosts morale and encourages continued high performance.

9. **Regular Team Check-Ins:**

- Conduct regular team meetings to discuss progress, challenges, and upcoming tasks.
- This ensures everyone is on the same page and can address any issues promptly.

10. **Continuous Improvement:**

- Encourage a culture of continuous improvement.
- Regularly review processes, gather feedback, and implement changes to enhance efficiency.

11. **Clear Roles and Responsibilities:**

- Define clear roles and responsibilities for each team member.
- Clarity helps avoid confusion and ensures that everyone knows what is expected of them.

12. **Encourage Skill Development:**

- Support ongoing skill development for team members.
- This not only enhances individual capabilities but also contributes to the overall strength of the team.

13. **Use Technology Wisely:**

- Leverage technology to automate repetitive tasks and streamline workflows.
- Implement tools that enhance collaboration, communication, and overall efficiency.

14. **Promote a Positive Team Culture:**

- Foster a positive and inclusive team culture.
- A supportive environment encourages creativity, innovation, and a sense of belonging.

15. **Regularly Evaluate and Adjust:**

- Regularly evaluate team processes and productivity.
- Be willing to adjust strategies based on feedback and evolving business needs.

By implementing these best practices, teams can create a productive and collaborative work environment, leading to enhanced efficiency and successful outcomes.

CHAPTER 5

GOOGLE CALENDAR AND MEET

- **Navigating Google Calendar**

Google Calendar is a powerful tool for managing schedules, appointments, and events. Here's a guide on navigating and using Google Calendar effectively:

1. **Accessing Google Calendar:**

- Open Google Calendar by navigating to calendar.google.com or clicking on the Calendar icon in your Google Apps menu.

2. **View Modes:**

- Use different view modes to suit your needs:
  - **Day:** Detailed view of a single day.
  - **Week:** Overview of a week's schedule.
  - **Month:** Calendar view for an entire month.
  - **Year:** A bird's eye view of the entire year.

3. **Creating Events:**

- Click on a specific date and time to create a new event.

- Provide details such as event title, location, start/end times, and any additional notes.

4. **Event Details and Reminders:**

- Customize event details, including color-coding for easy identification.
- Set reminders and notifications to receive alerts before the event starts.

5. **Recurring Events:**

- Easily create recurring events for daily, weekly, monthly, or custom schedules.
- Adjust the recurrence pattern based on your needs.

6. **Inviting Guests:**

- Invite others to your events by adding their email addresses.
- Guests receive invitations and can RSVP directly through Google Calendar.

7. **Calendar Sharing:**

- Share your calendar with specific people or make it public.
- Customize permissions to control who can view or edit your calendar.

8. **Integration with Gmail and Google Meet:**

- View and respond to event invitations directly from your Gmail inbox.
- Schedule Google Meet video calls directly from Google Calendar.

9. **Time Zones:**

- Easily switch between time zones to coordinate with individuals in different locations.
- Set your default time zone for accurate scheduling.

10. **Search and Filters:**

- Use the search bar to quickly find specific events.
- Apply filters to display events from specific calendars or categories.

11. **Custom Calendars and Colors:**

- Create multiple calendars for different aspects of your life (work, personal, etc.).
- Assign distinct colors to each calendar for easy identification.

12. **Drag-and-Drop Editing:**

- Drag and drop events to reschedule or change their duration.

- Adjusting events in this way automatically updates the event details.

13. **Mobile App Integration:**

- Access your calendar on the go through the Google Calendar mobile app.
- Sync events seamlessly between devices.

14. **Time Blocking:**

- Utilize time-blocking techniques to allocate specific time slots for tasks or activities.
- Enhance time management by visually organizing your day.

15. **Keyboard Shortcuts:**

- Speed up navigation using keyboard shortcuts (e.g., "C" to create a new event, "D" for day view, "W" for week view).

By mastering these navigation tips and features, you can make the most of Google Calendar to organize your schedule, collaborate with others, and manage your time effectively.

- **Scheduling Meetings with Google Meet**

Scheduling meetings with Google Meet is an efficient way to plan virtual gatherings, whether for work or personal reasons. Here's a guide on how to schedule and manage meetings using Google Meet:

1. **Accessing Google Meet:**

- Open Google Meet by visiting meet.google.com or accessing it through Google Calendar.

2. **Creating a Meeting through Google Calendar:**

- Open Google Calendar at calendar.google.com.
- Click on the "+ Create" button on the left side to create a new event.

3. **Adding Google Meet to an Event:**

- In the event details, click on "Add Google Meet video conferencing."
- A meeting link is automatically generated and added to the event.

4. **Setting Date and Time:**

- Choose the date and time for your meeting.
- Adjust the time zone as needed to accommodate participants in different locations.

5. **Adding Guests:**

- Invite participants to the meeting by adding their email addresses in the "Add guests" field.

- They will receive invitations with the meeting link.

6. **Adding Event Details:**

- Enter event details such as the meeting agenda, location, and any additional notes.

7. **Setting Notifications and Reminders:**

- Configure notifications and reminders to ensure participants are aware of the upcoming meeting.
- Google Calendar can send email reminders and pop-up notifications.

8. **Customizing Meeting Options:**

- Click on "More options" to access additional settings.
- Customize meeting options, such as guest permissions, event color, and visibility.

9. **Save and Send Invitations:**

- Save the event, and Google Calendar will send invitations to all invited participants.
- Invitations include the meeting link, which participants can use to join the meeting.

10. **Accessing the Meeting Link:**

- The meeting link is available within the event details on Google Calendar.
- Participants can click on the link to join the meeting directly.

11. **Starting the Meeting:**

- At the scheduled time, click on the meeting link to enter the virtual meeting room.
- Alternatively, participants can join the meeting by clicking on the link in the calendar event.

12. **Presenting and Screen Sharing:**

- The meeting host can present their screen or specific applications.
- Use the screen share option to showcase documents, presentations, or websites.

13. **Managing Participants:**

- Hosts can manage participants, mute/unmute attendees, and control access to the meeting.
- Participants can use the chat function to communicate during the meeting.

14. **Recording Meetings:**

- The meeting host can record the session for future reference.
- Recorded meetings are saved to Google Drive for easy access and sharing.

15. **Ending the Meeting:**

- Once the meeting is complete, click on the "End meeting" button.
- Participants will be disconnected, and the meeting link remains accessible for future use.

By utilizing Google Meet in conjunction with Google Calendar, you can seamlessly schedule, manage, and conduct virtual meetings with ease. The integration between these tools streamlines the process, providing a comprehensive solution for virtual collaboration.

- **Calendar Sharing and Permissions**

Calendar sharing and permissions in Google Calendar enable effective collaboration and coordination of schedules among individuals and teams. Here's a guide on how to share calendars and manage permissions:

1. **Accessing Calendar Sharing Settings:**

- Open Google Calendar at calendar.google.com.
- On the left sidebar, find the calendar you want to share and click on the three dots (More options) next to it.
- Select "Settings and sharing."

2. **Sharing with Specific People:**

- Under "Share with specific people," enter the email addresses of individuals you want to share the calendar with.
- Choose their permission level: "See only free/busy," "See all event details," or "Make changes to events."

3. **Making a Calendar Public:**

- Click on "Make available to public" if you want to allow anyone with the link to see your calendar's free/busy information.
- Set the level of detail to either "See only free/busy" or "See all event details."

4. **Adjusting Default Permissions:**

- Set default permissions for all new events created on the calendar.
- This is useful for maintaining consistent access levels for future events.

5. **Customizing Permissions for Specific Events:**

- When creating or editing an event, you can customize the permissions for that specific event.
- This is helpful when you need to share specific details or keep certain events private.

6. **Calendar Color Codes:**

- Each calendar can have a unique color.
- Customize colors for shared calendars to easily identify events from different sources.

7. **Viewing Shared Calendars:**

- Shared calendars appear on the left sidebar under "Other calendars."
- Toggle visibility on or off to control which calendars are displayed.

8. **Removing Calendar Access:**

- To stop sharing a calendar with someone, return to the "Settings and sharing" section.
- Click on the person's name under "Share with specific people" and select "Remove Access."

9. **Responding to Calendar Invitations:**

- When someone shares a calendar with you, you'll receive an invitation email.
- Accept the invitation to add the shared calendar to your list.

10. **Sharing on Mobile Devices:**

- Calendar sharing and permissions can be managed on mobile devices through the Google Calendar app.
- Access the app settings to control sharing preferences.

11. **Integration with Google Workspace:**

- In a business or educational setting, Google Calendar seamlessly integrates with Google Workspace.
- Permissions can be managed centrally, ensuring consistency across the organization.

12. **Collaboration with Shared Calendars:**

- Shared calendars are invaluable for team collaboration, project planning, and coordinating schedules.
- Team members can view, edit, and contribute to shared events based on their permissions.

By effectively managing calendar sharing and permissions, you can streamline collaboration, enhance communication, and ensure that everyone has the right level of access to relevant schedule information.

- **Mobile Calendar and Meet Features**

Google Calendar and Google Meet offer a range of features on mobile devices, providing flexibility and convenience for users who are on the go. Here's a guide to mobile calendar and Meet features:

Google Calendar Mobile Features:

1. **Mobile App Accessibility:**

- Access Google Calendar on mobile devices through the dedicated Google Calendar app (available for both Android and iOS).

2. **Quick Event Creation:**

- Create events on the go by tapping the "+" button.
- Enter event details, set reminders, and invite guests directly from your mobile device.

3. **Integration with Google Maps:**

- Calendar events can include location information with integration with Google Maps.

- Get directions and travel time estimates directly from the event details.

4. **Real-Time Notifications:**

- Receive real-time notifications for upcoming events and reminders.
- Customize notification settings to suit your preferences.

5. **Mobile Event Editing:**

- Easily edit event details, change dates, or add notes directly from the mobile app.
- Changes made on mobile are synced across all devices.

6. **Mobile View Modes:**

- Switch between daily, weekly, monthly, and schedule view modes to tailor your calendar display on smaller screens.

7. **Event Colors and Visibility:**

- Customize event colors and visibility settings on the mobile app.
- Maintain a visually organized calendar with personalized color-coding.

8. **Mobile Widgets:**

- Add Google Calendar widgets to your mobile device's home screen for quick access to upcoming events.

9. **Voice Commands:**

- Use voice commands to create, edit, or search for events using Google Assistant.
- Enable hands-free interaction with your calendar.

Google Meet Mobile Features:

1. **Mobile App Accessibility:**

- Access Google Meet on mobile devices through the dedicated Google Meet app (available for both Android and iOS).

2. **Scheduled Meeting Reminders:**

- Receive reminders for scheduled Google Meet meetings directly on your mobile device.
- Join meetings with a single tap from the notification.

3. **Joining Meetings on the Go:**

- Join video meetings from anywhere with just a tap on your mobile device.
- Use your phone's camera and microphone for video and audio.

4. **Screen Sharing:**

- Hosts can share their screens directly from the mobile app.
- Share presentations, documents, or any content during a meeting.

5. **Chat and Messaging:**

- Access the chat feature to send messages and links during a Google Meet session.
- Collaborate with participants through text while in the meeting.

6. **Adjustable Layouts:**

- Customize your video call layout based on your preference.
- Choose between grid view and active speaker view.

7. **Mobile Controls for Hosts:**

- Hosts have controls to manage participants, mute/unmute, and control meeting settings.
- Ensure smooth facilitation of the meeting from a mobile device.

8. **Integration with Google Calendar:**

- Google Meet seamlessly integrates with Google Calendar on mobile.
- Join meetings directly from calendar events.

9. **Mobile Background Blur:**

- Use the background blur feature to maintain privacy and focus during video calls.
- This feature helps keep the focus on you, not your surroundings.

10. **Low-Light Mode:**

- Automatically enhance video visibility in low-light conditions for a better viewing experience.

By leveraging these features on mobile devices, users can stay connected, manage their schedules, and participate in virtual meetings with ease, regardless of their location.

- **Efficient Time Management Tips**

Efficient time management is essential for productivity and work-life balance. Here are some tips to help you manage your time more effectively:

1. **Set Clear Goals:**

- Clearly define your short-term and long-term goals.

- Break down larger goals into smaller, manageable tasks.

2. **Prioritize Tasks:**

- Identify high-priority tasks and focus on them first.
- Use methods like the Eisenhower Matrix to categorize tasks by urgency and importance.

3. **Create a To-Do List:**

- Make a daily or weekly to-do list.
- Organize tasks by priority and allocate time to each.

4. **Time Blocking:**

- Allocate specific blocks of time for different activities.
- This helps create a structured schedule and minimizes multitasking.

5. **Use a Calendar:**

- Use a calendar tool to schedule appointments, meetings, and deadlines.
- Set reminders to stay on track.

6. **Eliminate Distractions:**

- Identify and minimize distractions in your workspace.

- Turn off non-essential notifications during focused work periods.

7. **Batch Similar Tasks:**

- Group similar tasks together and tackle them in batches.
- This minimizes context-switching and enhances efficiency.

8. **Set Time Limits:**

- Allocate a specific amount of time to each task.
- Use techniques like the Pomodoro Technique with focused work intervals and short breaks.

9. **Learn to Delegate:**

- Delegate tasks when possible.
- Focus on tasks that align with your strengths and expertise.

10. **Avoid Perfectionism:**

- Strive for excellence but avoid perfectionism.
- Recognize when a task is "good enough" to move on to the next one.

11. **Use Technology Wisely:**

- Leverage productivity tools and apps.

- Explore project management tools, time-tracking apps, and calendar apps.

12. **Regular Breaks:**

- Take regular breaks to refresh your mind.
- Short breaks can improve focus and prevent burnout.

13. **Learn to Say No:**

- Be selective about commitments.
- Politely decline tasks that don't align with your priorities.

14. **Reflect and Learn:**

- Periodically review your time management strategies.
- Identify areas for improvement and adjust your approach accordingly.

15. **Maintain Work-Life Balance:**

- Set boundaries between work and personal life.
- Allocate time for relaxation, hobbies, and spending time with loved ones.

16. **Continuous Learning:**

- Invest time in learning new skills and techniques.

- Stay updated on time management strategies and productivity methods.

17. **Mindfulness and Focus:**

- Practice mindfulness to stay present in the moment.
- Cultivate deep work by minimizing distractions and focusing on the task at hand.

18. **Regular Evaluations:**

- Regularly assess your goals and progress.
- Adjust your strategies based on changing priorities and circumstances.

19. **Celebrate Achievements:**

- Acknowledge and celebrate your accomplishments.
- Positive reinforcement can boost motivation.

20. **Get Adequate Sleep:**

- Ensure you get sufficient, quality sleep.
- Sleep is crucial for cognitive function and overall well-being.

By incorporating these time management tips into your daily routine, you can enhance your productivity, reduce stress, and achieve a better balance between work and personal life.

CHAPTER 6

COMMUNICATION WITH GOOGLE CHAT AND SPACES

- **Introduction to Google Chat**

Google Chat is a communication platform developed by Google, providing users with a versatile and collaborative way to connect with colleagues, friends, or groups. Here's an introduction to Google Chat:

1. **Purpose and Functionality:**

- Google Chat serves as a messaging platform designed for both one-on-one and group conversations.
- It is part of the Google Workspace suite, offering seamless integration with other Google apps and services.

2. **Integration with Google Workspace:**

- Google Chat is tightly integrated with other Google Workspace applications, such as Gmail, Google Drive, and Google Calendar.
- Users can transition seamlessly from chat conversations to collaborative document editing or video meetings.

3. **Real-Time Messaging:**

- Engage in real-time text-based conversations with individuals or groups.
- Chat supports instant messaging, making it a quick and efficient communication tool.

4. **Group Conversations and Rooms:**

- Create group conversations or rooms to facilitate discussions among teams or project groups.
- Rooms provide a centralized space for ongoing collaboration and file sharing.

5. **File Sharing and Collaboration:**

- Share files directly within the chat interface.
- Collaborate on Google Drive documents, sheets, or slides without leaving the conversation.

6. **Notification Controls:**

- Customize notification settings for individual chats or rooms.
- Choose to receive notifications for all messages, mentions, or specific keywords.

7. **Mentions and Replies:**

- Mention specific users in a conversation using the "@" symbol followed by their name.
- Reply directly to messages to maintain organized and threaded conversations.

8. **Direct Integration with Google Meet:**

- Initiate Google Meet video calls directly from a chat conversation or room.
- Seamlessly transition from text-based communication to face-to-face meetings.

9. **Search and History:**

- Easily search for specific messages or content within the chat history.
- Access a comprehensive history of your conversations.

10. **Access Across Devices:**

- Use Google Chat on various devices, including desktops, laptops, tablets, and mobile phones.
- Sync conversations and stay connected regardless of your device.

11. **Bot Integration:**

- Integrate bots to automate tasks or provide information within the chat.
- Bots can offer updates, answer queries, or perform specific actions.

12. **Security and Compliance:**

- Google Chat prioritizes security, offering features such as end-to-end encryption and compliance with industry standards.
- Users can confidently communicate sensitive information within the platform.

13. **Status Indicators:**

- View the online or offline status of your contacts.
- Presence indicators help you know when colleagues are available for communication.

14. **Access Controls:**

- Admins have control over user access and permissions.
- Implement access controls to ensure secure and authorized use of Google Chat.

15. **Custom Emojis and Reactions:**

- Use custom emojis and reactions to express emotions or reactions in the chat.
- Enhance the conversational experience with visual elements.

Google Chat enhances collaboration and communication within organizations, offering a dynamic and integrated platform for team discussions, file sharing, and seamless integration with other Google Workspace applications.

- **Collaborative Messaging in Spaces**

Collaborative messaging in Google Chat is facilitated through spaces, which are dedicated areas for team discussions, project coordination, and group collaboration. Here's an overview of collaborative messaging in spaces within Google Chat:

1. **Creation of Spaces:**

- Spaces are created to bring together individuals or teams for collaborative discussions.
- Users can create spaces for specific projects, departments, or ongoing conversations.

2. **Group and Direct Messages:**

- Spaces allow for both group messages involving multiple participants and direct messages for one-on-one conversations.
- Participants can easily switch between group discussions and private conversations within the same space.

3. **Threaded Conversations:**

- Conversations in spaces are organized in threaded discussions.
- Threads help maintain context and keep related messages together, facilitating focused communication.

4. **Mentions and Notifications:**

- Users can mention specific individuals in a space using the "@" symbol followed by their name.
- Notifications are generated for mentions, ensuring that relevant participants are aware of the message.

5. **File Sharing and Collaboration:**

- Spaces facilitate seamless file sharing and collaboration.
- Participants can share documents, spreadsheets, presentations, or any other files directly within the space.

6. **Integrations with Google Workspace:**

- Spaces integrate with other Google Workspace applications, such as Google Drive and Google Calendar.
- Users can collaborate on shared documents and schedule events without leaving the chat interface.

7. **Access Controls:**

- Administrators and space owners can define access controls and permissions for spaces.
- This ensures that only authorized individuals can access and participate in specific spaces.

8. **Google Meet Integration:**

- Spaces seamlessly integrate with Google Meet for video conferencing.
- Users can initiate video meetings directly from a space, enhancing real-time collaboration.

9. **Search and History:**

- Spaces maintain a searchable history of conversations.
- Users can quickly locate past discussions, making it easy to reference and retrieve information.

10. **Task and Action Items:**

- Spaces can be used to assign tasks and action items to team members.
- Participants can discuss, plan, and track progress on tasks within the space.

11. **Bot Integrations:**

- Bots can be integrated into spaces to automate tasks, provide updates, or offer specific information.
- Bots enhance the functionality of spaces and streamline collaborative workflows.

12. **Status Updates:**

- Participants can update their status to indicate availability or provide context to their current activities.
- Status indicators help teams understand each other's availability for communication.

13. **Customization and Theming:**

- Spaces can be customized with themes and visual elements.
- Customization options allow teams to personalize their collaborative environment.

14. **Cross-Platform Accessibility:**

- Google Chat, including spaces, is accessible across various platforms, including desktops, laptops, tablets, and mobile devices.

- Users can participate in collaborative messaging from their preferred devices.

15. **Real-Time Editing and Responses:**

- Participants can collaborate in real-time on shared documents within a space.

- Responses and edits are visible instantly, promoting efficient and dynamic collaboration.

Google Chat spaces provide a comprehensive platform for collaborative messaging, integrating various communication tools and features to streamline teamwork and enhance productivity within organizations.

- **Real-time Communication Features**

Real-time communication features in Google Chat enhance the speed and efficiency of collaborative efforts. Here's an overview of the real-time communication features available:

1. **Instant Messaging:**

- Google Chat provides instant messaging capabilities for real-time communication.
- Participants can exchange text messages, facilitating quick and direct conversations.

2. **Mentions and Notifications:**

- Users can mention specific individuals in a message using the "@" symbol followed by their name.
- Mentions trigger notifications, ensuring that the relevant participants are alerted to the message.

3. **Read Receipts:**

- Read receipts indicate when a message has been read by the recipient.
- This feature helps users track the status of their messages and gauge response times.

4. **Real-Time Typing Indicators:**

- Typing indicators show when someone is actively typing a message.
- This feature provides real-time awareness of ongoing communication and responses.

5. **Live Presence Indicators:**

- Presence indicators display the online or offline status of users.
- Participants can see whether their colleagues are currently available for communication.

6. **Real-Time Collaboration on Documents:**

- Spaces and direct messages support real-time collaboration on shared documents.
- Multiple users can edit documents simultaneously, with changes visible to all participants in real time.

7. **Google Meet Integration:**

- Seamless integration with Google Meet allows users to initiate video meetings directly from the chat interface.
- Users can transition from text-based communication to face-to-face discussions in real time.

8. **Live Reaction Emojis:**

- Participants can use live reaction emojis to express immediate reactions to messages.
- Emojis provide a quick and visual way to convey sentiments in real-time conversations.

9. **Real-Time File Sharing:**

- Users can share files in real time within a chat or space.
- Shared files are accessible to participants instantly, promoting efficient collaboration.

10. **Live Updates and Notifications:**

- Receive live updates and notifications for new messages or mentions.
- Notifications ensure that users stay informed about ongoing conversations.

11. **Interactive Threads:**

- Threads within spaces allow for organized and interactive discussions.
- Participants can respond to specific messages within a thread, maintaining context.

12. **Mobile Accessibility:**

- Real-time communication is accessible on mobile devices through the Google Chat mobile app.
- Participants can stay connected and engage in conversations while on the go.

13. **Bot Integrations for Automation:**

- Bots can be integrated to automate tasks and provide real-time updates.
- Automated responses and notifications enhance the speed of information dissemination.

14. **Cross-Platform Synchronization:**

- Real-time communication is synchronized across various platforms, ensuring consistency.
- Messages and updates made on one device are reflected in real time on other connected devices.

15. **Responsive Design:**

- The user interface of Google Chat is designed for responsiveness, providing a smooth and real-time experience.
- The platform adapts to different screen sizes and resolutions.

These real-time communication features in Google Chat contribute to a dynamic and collaborative environment, enabling teams to stay connected, share information, and make decisions in real time.

- **Integrating Chat and Email**

Integrating Google Chat and Gmail provides a seamless communication experience, allowing users to transition effortlessly between chat conversations and email correspondence. Here's how you can leverage the integration between Google Chat and Gmail:

1. **Chat in Gmail Sidebar:**

- Access Google Chat directly within the Gmail sidebar.
- The sidebar displays a list of your recent chat conversations, making it convenient to switch between email and chat.

2. **Chat and Email Labels:**

- Conversations in Google Chat are labeled similarly to emails, ensuring consistency.
- Labels help organize and categorize your communication, making it easy to locate specific chats or emails.

3. **Chat Notifications in Gmail:**

- Receive chat notifications directly within Gmail.
- Notifications alert you to new messages, mentions, or replies in real time.

4. **One-click Access to Chat:**

- Initiate chat conversations with your contacts directly from Gmail.
- Click on a contact's profile picture in the sidebar to start a chat without leaving the email interface.

5. **Switch Between Email and Chat Tabs:**

- Toggle between the "Mail" and "Chat" tabs in Gmail to switch between email and chat views.
- This provides a flexible and intuitive way to manage your communications.

6. **Email to Chat Conversion:**

- Easily transition from an email conversation to a chat by clicking on the chat icon within an email.
- This allows for real-time collaboration on specific topics.

7. **Chat History in Gmail:**

- View your chat history directly within Gmail.
- The chat history provides a chronological record of your conversations, similar to email threads.

8. **Integration with Google Meet:**

- Schedule and start Google Meet video calls directly from Gmail.
- The integration streamlines the process of transitioning from email or chat to face-to-face meetings.

9. **Unified Search Across Email and Chat:**

- Use the unified search bar in Gmail to search for both emails and chat conversations.
- Search results include relevant emails and chat messages, providing a comprehensive view of communication.

10. **Shared Contacts Between Email and Chat:**

- Contacts are shared between Gmail and Chat, ensuring consistency.
- Changes to contact details are reflected in both email and chat interfaces.

11. **Read and Unread Status Sync:**

- Read and unread statuses are synchronized between email and chat.
- Marking a message as read or unread in one interface is reflected in the other.

12. **Smart Replies and Suggestions:**

- Smart replies and suggestions are available in both email and chat.
- Google's AI suggests quick responses, enhancing communication efficiency.

13. **Attachment Sharing Across Platforms:**

- Attachments can be shared seamlessly between Gmail and Chat.
- Shared files in one platform are accessible in the other, promoting collaborative document editing.

14. **Cross-Platform Accessibility:**

- Access both Gmail and Chat on various devices, including desktops, laptops, tablets, and mobile phones.
- Synchronization ensures a consistent experience across platforms.

15. **Collaborative Document Editing:**

- Collaborate on Google Docs, Sheets, or Slides directly from Gmail or Chat.
- Shared documents are accessible and editable in real time by all collaborators.

By integrating Google Chat and Gmail, users can benefit from a unified communication experience, allowing for efficient collaboration, easy access to conversations, and a seamless transition between email and chat interactions.

- **Best Practices for Effective Communication**

Effective communication is crucial for successful collaboration and productivity. Here are some best practices to enhance your communication skills:

1. **Clarity and Conciseness:**

- Clearly articulate your message and avoid unnecessary details.
- Use concise language to convey your point effectively.

2. **Active Listening:**

- Listen attentively to others without interrupting.
- Confirm your understanding by paraphrasing or summarizing what you've heard.

3. **Choose the Right Medium:**

- Select the most appropriate communication channel for your message.

- Consider factors such as urgency, complexity, and the nature of the information.

4. **Be Mindful of Tone:**

- Choose a tone that matches the context and audience.
- Be mindful of the impact of your words on the receiver.

5. **Use Clear and Specific Language:**

- Avoid vague or ambiguous language.
- Clearly state your expectations and provide specific details.

6. **Empathy and Emotional Intelligence:**

- Understand and acknowledge the emotions of others.
- Approach conversations with empathy and emotional intelligence.

7. **Ask for Feedback:**

- Encourage feedback from others to ensure mutual understanding.
- Use feedback as an opportunity for improvement.

8. **Use Visuals to Support Communication:**

- Incorporate visuals like charts or graphs to enhance understanding.

- Visual aids can clarify complex information.

9. **Consider Cultural Differences:**

- Be aware of cultural nuances that may affect communication.
- Adapt your communication style to be inclusive and respectful.

10. **Provide Context:**

- Offer sufficient background information to help others understand the context.
- Contextual information enhances comprehension.

11. **Timely Responses:**

- Respond promptly to messages and inquiries.
- Communicate delays and set realistic expectations for response times.

12. **Avoid Jargon:**

- Minimize the use of industry-specific jargon.
- Use language that is easily understood by your audience.

13. **Use Positive Language:**

- Frame messages in a positive and constructive manner.

- Focus on solutions rather than problems.

14. **Follow Up:**

- Follow up on important discussions to ensure understanding.
- Summarize key points and confirm action items.

15. **Mindful Use of Email:**

- Keep email communication clear and to the point.
- Use subject lines effectively and avoid unnecessary CCs.

16. **Be Open to Questions:**

- Encourage questions and provide clarifications when needed.
- Foster an open and collaborative environment.

17. **Practice Constructive Criticism:**

- If offering criticism, do so constructively and provide solutions.
- Frame feedback in a way that promotes growth and improvement.

18. **Understand Non-Verbal Cues:**

- Pay attention to non-verbal cues such as body language and facial expressions.

- Non-verbal communication can convey additional information.

19. **Use Technology Wisely:**

- Leverage communication tools effectively.
- Choose the right platforms for different types of communication.

20. **Continuous Improvement:**

- Reflect on your communication style and seek areas for improvement.
- Embrace a mindset of continuous learning and adaptation.

By incorporating these best practices into your communication habits, you can foster a more collaborative and positive work environment, leading to better understanding, increased productivity, and stronger team dynamics.

CHAPTER 7

SECURITY AND PRIVACY IN GOOGLE WORKSPACE

- **Google Workspace Security Features**

Google Workspace provides robust security features to protect user data, maintain privacy, and ensure the integrity of communication and collaboration tools. Here are key security features offered by Google Workspace:

1. **Two-Factor Authentication (2FA):**

- Enhance account security by enabling two-factor authentication.
- Users must provide a second verification step, such as a code from a mobile app, in addition to their password.

2. **Data Encryption:**

- Data transmission between users and Google servers is encrypted using Transport Layer Security (TLS).
- Emails, documents, and other files stored in Google Drive are encrypted at rest.

3. **Identity and Access Management:**

- Admins can manage user access and permissions through the Admin Console.
- Implement least privilege principles to restrict access to sensitive data.

4. **Mobile Device Management (MDM):**

- Admins can enforce security policies on mobile devices accessing Google Workspace.
- Features include device passcode requirements, encryption, and remote device wiping.

5. **Security Key Enforcement:**

- Require the use of physical security keys for added authentication.
- This provides an additional layer of protection against unauthorized access.

6. **Advanced Phishing Protection:**

- Google Workspace employs machine learning to detect and prevent phishing attacks.
- Suspicious emails are flagged, and users are warned of potential risks.

7. **Data Loss Prevention (DLP):**

- Admins can configure DLP policies to prevent the sharing of sensitive information.
- Policies can identify and block the transmission of specific data types, such as credit card numbers or social security numbers.

8. **Security Center:**

- The Security Center provides a unified dashboard for monitoring and managing security settings.
- Admins can gain insights into potential security threats and take action to address them.

9. **Audit Logging and Reporting:**

- Audit logs provide a record of user activity within Google Workspace.
- Admins can review logs to identify security incidents, unauthorized access, or policy violations.

10. **Endpoint Verification:**

- Verify the security status of devices accessing Google Workspace.
- Admins can assess the security posture of endpoints and enforce compliance policies.

11. **Safe Browsing:**

- Google Workspace integrates with Google Safe Browsing to protect users from malicious websites and phishing attempts.
- URLs are checked in real time to ensure they are safe to access.

12. **App Access Controls:**

- Admins can manage third-party app access to Google Workspace data.
- Control which apps can access user data and enforce security policies.

13. **Incident Response:**

- Google Workspace provides incident response capabilities to help organizations handle security incidents.
- Admins can investigate and remediate security issues effectively.

14. **Security Notifications:**

- Admins and users receive security notifications for critical events, such as suspicious login attempts.
- Immediate alerts help users take action to secure their accounts.

15. **Compliance and Certifications:**

- Google Workspace complies with various industry standards and certifications, such as ISO 27001, SOC 2, and HIPAA.
- This ensures that the service meets rigorous security and privacy standards.

16. **Security Checkup:**

- Users can perform a Security Checkup to review and enhance the security of their Google accounts.
- The Checkup covers account recovery options, recent security events, and third-party access.

17. **Continuous Security Updates:**

- Google Workspace receives regular security updates and improvements.
- This ensures that the service remains resilient against evolving security threats.

By leveraging these security features, organizations using Google Workspace can create a secure and protected environment for their communication, collaboration, and data storage needs. Admins play a crucial role in configuring and managing these features to align with organizational security policies and requirements.

- **Privacy Settings and Controls**

Google Workspace provides users with a range of privacy settings and controls to manage how their data is handled and shared. Here are key privacy settings and controls available in Google Workspace:

1. **Privacy Dashboard:**

- Users can access the Privacy Dashboard to review and manage their privacy settings.
- The dashboard provides an overview of the user's privacy and security settings across various Google services.

2. **Account Permissions:**

- Users can review and manage third-party apps with access to their Google account.
- Control which apps have permission to access data and revoke access when necessary.

3. **Ad Personalization Settings:**

- Users can control the personalization of ads based on their interests.
- Adjust ad settings to limit the data used for ad personalization.

4. **Activity Controls:**

- Activity Controls allow users to manage and control their Google activity data.
- Users can enable or disable various activity settings, including web and app activity, location history, and device information.

5. **Location Sharing Settings:**

- Users can control who can see their location and manage location sharing settings.
- Choose between sharing location with specific individuals, sharing only city-level location, or disabling location sharing.

6. **Google Photos Privacy Controls:**

- Users can manage privacy settings for Google Photos, controlling who can see and interact with their photos.
- Adjust sharing settings for individual albums or photos.

7. **Drive and Docs Privacy Settings:**

- Control the sharing settings for files and folders in Google Drive.

- Set permissions to limit access to specific individuals or groups.

8. **Calendar Privacy Settings:**

- Users can manage privacy settings for their Google Calendar.
- Control who can see their calendar events and adjust sharing settings for specific events.

9. **Email Privacy Settings:**

- Manage email privacy settings, including who can send emails and view contact details.
- Adjust settings to control the visibility of your online status.

10. **Hangouts Chat Privacy Controls:**

- Adjust privacy settings in Hangouts Chat to control who can contact you and see your status.
- Manage notifications and decide whether to show your online status.

11. **Profile Information Visibility:**

- Users can control the visibility of their profile information.

- Adjust settings to determine who can see details like your profile picture, name, and email address.

12. **Shared Device Settings:**

- Manage settings for shared devices, including Smart Lock for Android devices.
- Control which devices are considered trusted and can access your Google account without additional authentication.

13. **YouTube Privacy Controls:**

- Control privacy settings for YouTube activities.
- Adjust settings for video recommendations, search history, and comments.

14. **Incognito Mode:**

- Use Incognito mode in Google Chrome to browse without saving your browsing history.
- This mode ensures that your searches and visited websites are not stored locally.

15. **Data Retention Policies:**

- Admins can configure data retention policies for Google Workspace.
- Set policies to control how long data is retained in services like Gmail and Drive.

16. **Google Meet Privacy Controls:**

- Users can control privacy settings for Google Meet, including who can join their meetings.
- Adjust settings to restrict meeting access to specific individuals or groups.

17. **Workspace Security Key:**

- Users can enhance account security by using a security key for two-factor authentication.
- Security keys provide an additional layer of protection against unauthorized access.

By actively managing these privacy settings and controls, users can customize their Google Workspace experience to align with their preferences and ensure that their data is handled in accordance with their privacy preferences. Admins play a crucial role in configuring organizational-level privacy settings and educating users on best practices for privacy management.

- **Data Backup and Recovery**

Data backup and recovery are essential components of a robust data management strategy, ensuring that critical information is protected against loss and can be restored in case of unforeseen events. In Google Workspace, several features and practices contribute to effective data backup and recovery:

1. **Google Vault:**

- Google Vault is a data archiving and e-discovery solution that allows organizations to retain, search, and export specific data.
- It provides a centralized platform for managing and securing valuable information.

2. **Backup and Sync:**

- Users can utilize Google's Backup and Sync tool to back up their files and folders from their desktop to Google Drive.
- This ensures that important documents, images, and other files are stored securely in the cloud.

3. **Google Drive Version History:**

- Google Drive maintains version history for documents, spreadsheets, and other files.
- Users can review and restore previous versions of a file, providing a built-in mechanism for data recovery.

4. **Google Admin Console:**

- Admins have access to the Google Admin Console, where they can configure and manage data backup and recovery policies.

- This includes setting retention policies, controlling data access, and managing user accounts.

5. **Data Export:**

- Google Workspace allows users to export their data, including emails, contacts, and files.
- This export functionality can be valuable for creating local backups or transitioning to a different platform.

6. **Third-Party Backup Solutions:**

- Organizations can explore third-party backup solutions that specialize in Google Workspace data protection.
- These solutions often offer additional features, such as automated backups, granular recovery options, and enhanced security.

7. **Team Drives:**

- Team Drives in Google Drive provide a collaborative space for teams to store and share files.
- Admins can manage access and permissions, ensuring that important team data is protected.

8. **Email Archiving:**

- Google Vault can be used for email archiving, allowing organizations to retain and search email data for compliance and legal purposes.

- It provides a centralized repository for managing email archives.

9. **Data Loss Prevention (DLP):**

- Google Workspace includes DLP features to prevent the accidental sharing of sensitive information.

- DLP policies can be configured to protect data across various services, reducing the risk of data loss.

10. **Regular Backups of Configuration Settings:**

- Admins should regularly back up configuration settings in the Google Admin Console.

- This ensures that important settings and policies can be restored in case of configuration changes or system failures.

11. **Security Best Practices:**

- Implement security best practices to minimize the risk of data loss.

- This includes educating users on safe computing practices, enforcing strong authentication, and regularly updating security measures.

12. **Testing Recovery Processes:**

- Regularly test data recovery processes to ensure that backups are functional and can be successfully restored.
- This proactive approach helps identify and address any potential issues before they become critical.

13. **Monitoring and Alerts:**

- Set up monitoring and alerts to detect unusual activities or potential data loss events.
- Timely alerts enable quick response and minimize the impact of data loss incidents.

14. **Offline Access and Sync:**

- Encourage users to enable offline access and synchronization for critical files.
- This ensures that essential documents are accessible even in situations where an internet connection is not available.

By implementing these practices and utilizing the built-in features of Google Workspace, organizations can establish a comprehensive approach to data backup and recovery. This approach helps protect against data loss, supports compliance requirements, and ensures business continuity.

- **Compliance and Governance**

Ensuring compliance and governance within Google Workspace is crucial for organizations to meet legal, regulatory, and internal requirements. Here are key considerations and features for maintaining compliance and governance:

1. **Data Ownership and Access Controls:**

- Clearly define data ownership and access controls within the organization.

- Use the Google Admin Console to manage user access and permissions, ensuring the principle of least privilege.

2. **Compliance Center:**

- Google Workspace provides a Compliance Center where admins can configure and manage compliance settings.

- Admins can set up data loss prevention (DLP) policies, retention rules, and e-discovery for legal and compliance purposes.

3. **Data Classification and Sensitivity Labels:**

- Implement data classification and sensitivity labels to identify and protect sensitive information.

- Apply labels to emails, documents, and other files to enforce security and compliance policies.

4. **Data Retention Policies:**

- Configure data retention policies in the Google Admin Console to determine how long data is retained in services like Gmail and Google Drive.

- Establish policies that align with regulatory requirements and organizational needs.

5. **E-Discovery with Google Vault:**

- Google Vault allows organizations to retain, search, and export data for legal and compliance purposes.

- Conduct e-discovery searches across Gmail, Drive, and other Google Workspace services.

6. **Audit Logging:**

- Enable and review audit logs to track user activity within Google Workspace.

- Admins can monitor actions such as logins, file accesses, and permission changes to ensure compliance.

7. **Third-Party Audits and Certifications:**

- Google Workspace undergoes third-party audits and certifications to demonstrate compliance with industry standards.

- These certifications may include ISO 27001, SOC 2, HIPAA, and others, depending on the organizational requirements.

8. **Legal Holds:**

- Place legal holds on specific data to prevent its deletion during investigations or legal proceedings.
- Google Vault provides the capability to enforce legal holds on relevant data.

9. **Access Reviews:**

- Conduct regular access reviews to ensure that user access aligns with business requirements and compliance policies.
- Admins can use the Google Admin Console to review and manage user permissions.

10. **Security Best Practices:**

- Implement security best practices to protect sensitive data.
- This includes enforcing strong authentication, educating users on security awareness, and regularly updating security measures.

11. **Incident Response Plan:**

- Develop and maintain an incident response plan to address security incidents promptly.

- Clearly define roles, responsibilities, and communication protocols to handle incidents effectively.

12. **User Training and Awareness:**

- Conduct regular training sessions to educate users about compliance requirements and best practices.
- Ensure that users understand their responsibilities regarding data handling and security.

13. **Collaboration with Legal and Compliance Teams:**

- Foster collaboration between IT teams, legal departments, and compliance teams.
- Ensure that IT policies align with legal and regulatory requirements.

14. **Data Transfer Controls:**

- Implement controls for data transfer, especially for organizations operating in regions with specific data residency requirements.
- Ensure that data is transferred and stored in compliance with applicable regulations.

15. **Vendor Management:**

- If using third-party apps or services within Google Workspace, assess their compliance and security posture.

- Ensure that third-party tools adhere to the organization's compliance standards.

16. **Regular Compliance Audits:**

- Conduct regular internal and external compliance audits to assess adherence to policies and regulations.
- Use the findings to make improvements and address potential compliance gaps.

By implementing these measures, organizations can establish a strong compliance and governance framework within Google Workspace. This framework helps protect sensitive information, ensures legal and regulatory adherence, and promotes a secure and transparent operational environment.

- **User Training and Awareness**

User training and awareness are integral components of a robust cybersecurity strategy within Google Workspace. Educating users helps them understand potential risks, adopt security best practices, and contribute to a secure digital environment. Here are key elements to consider when designing user training and awareness programs:

1. **Security Policy Awareness:**

- Ensure that users are familiar with the organization's security policies and guidelines.

- Communicate clearly about acceptable use, data handling practices, and compliance requirements.

2. **Phishing Awareness:**

- Train users to recognize phishing attempts and suspicious emails.
- Conduct simulated phishing exercises to provide hands-on experience and reinforce awareness.

3. **Password Security:**

- Educate users on the importance of strong, unique passwords.
- Promote the use of password managers for secure password management.

4. **Multi-Factor Authentication (MFA):**

- Emphasize the benefits of multi-factor authentication.
- Guide users on how to enable and use MFA for an extra layer of account security.

5. **Device Security:**

- Provide guidance on securing devices, including laptops, smartphones, and tablets.

- Encourage regular software updates, device encryption, and the use of screen locks.

6. **Data Handling Best Practices:**

- Instruct users on how to handle sensitive data securely.
- Emphasize the importance of data classification, encryption, and secure file sharing practices.

7. **Google Workspace Features:**

- Conduct training sessions on Google Workspace features related to security and privacy.
- Highlight features such as sharing settings, version history, and security controls.

8. **Mobile Device Management (MDM):**

- If applicable, educate users on the organization's mobile device management policies.
- Instruct users on how to set up and use MDM features for enhanced mobile security.

9. **Social Engineering Awareness:**

- Raise awareness about social engineering tactics used by attackers.

- Provide examples of common social engineering techniques and how to avoid falling victim to them.

10. **Safe Browsing Practices:**

- Instruct users on safe browsing practices to avoid malicious websites.
- Encourage the use of secure connections (HTTPS) and caution against clicking on suspicious links.

11. **Incident Reporting:**

- Establish clear channels for reporting security incidents or suspicious activities.
- Train users on the importance of timely reporting to facilitate incident response.

12. **Regular Security Updates:**

- Keep users informed about the latest security threats and vulnerabilities.
- Provide regular updates on security best practices and emerging threats.

13. **Remote Work Security:**

- If applicable, provide specific guidance on securing remote work environments.

- Cover topics such as secure Wi-Fi usage, virtual private networks (VPNs), and home office security.

14. **Data Backup Procedures:**

- Educate users on the importance of regular data backups.
- Instruct them on how to use Google Workspace features for file versioning and recovery.

15. **Continuous Training:**

- Security awareness is an ongoing process. Conduct regular training sessions and refresher courses.
- Keep users informed about evolving cybersecurity threats and countermeasures.

16. **Collaboration and Communication Etiquette:**

- Promote professional and secure communication practices.
- Provide guidance on appropriate collaboration and file-sharing practices within Google Workspace.

17. **Feedback and Q&A Sessions:**

- Create opportunities for users to provide feedback and ask questions.

- Address common concerns and tailor training content based on user feedback.

18. **Reward and Recognition:**

- Implement a recognition program to acknowledge individuals or teams for practicing good security habits.
- Positive reinforcement can motivate users to actively participate in security initiatives.

19. **Use Case Scenarios:**

- Provide real-world use case scenarios to illustrate security concepts.
- Engage users with practical examples to enhance understanding.

20. **Integration with Onboarding:**

- Include security training as part of the onboarding process for new employees.
- Ensure that new hires receive comprehensive training on security policies and practices.

By incorporating these elements into user training and awareness programs, organizations can empower their users to become active participants in maintaining a secure and resilient digital environment within Google Workspace. Ongoing education and awareness efforts contribute significantly to the overall cybersecurity posture of the organization.

CONCLUSION

In conclusion, mastering Google Workspace requires a holistic approach that encompasses understanding the ecosystem, configuring settings, utilizing collaborative tools, ensuring security, and fostering a culture of compliance and awareness. The comprehensive guide outlined the following key aspects:

1. **Understanding the Ecosystem:**

- Delve into the fundamentals of Google Workspace, exploring its suite of collaborative applications and their interconnected functionalities.

2. **Setting Up Your Account:**

- Navigate through the process of creating and customizing your Google Workspace account to suit your organizational needs.

3. **Customizing Workspace Settings:**

- Tailor the settings within Google Workspace to optimize your user experience and align with your team's workflows.

4. **Exploring the Workspace Interface:**

- Familiarize yourself with the user interface of Google Workspace, enabling efficient navigation and utilization of its features.

5. **Accessing Help and Support:**

- Learn how to leverage the available help and support resources within Google Workspace to address queries and troubleshoot issues effectively.

6. **Email Basics and Management:**

- Dive into the essentials of Gmail, mastering email basics and effective management strategies for streamlined communication.

7. **Organizing with Labels and Filters:**

- Harness the power of labels and filters in Gmail to organize your inbox and enhance email management efficiency.

8. **Productivity Features in Gmail:**

- Explore advanced productivity features in Gmail, optimizing your email workflow and maximizing efficiency.

9. **Collaboration Tools in Gmail:**

- Unlock the collaborative potential of Gmail, utilizing tools and features that facilitate effective teamwork and communication.

10. **Advanced Tips and Tricks:**

- Elevate your proficiency by exploring advanced tips and tricks across various Google Workspace applications.

11. **Google Drive Basics:**

- Master the basics of Google Drive, understanding file organization, storage, and collaboration features.

12. **Collaborative Document Creation:**

- Learn how to create and collaborate on documents using Google Docs, fostering seamless teamwork and document editing.

13. **Spreadsheets in Google Sheets:**

- Dive into the world of Google Sheets, mastering spreadsheet creation, data manipulation, and collaborative analysis.

14. **Designing Presentations with Google Slides:**

- Explore the features of Google Slides to create visually appealing and engaging presentations for effective communication.

15. **Storing and Analyzing Data with Google Forms:**

- Utilize Google Forms for efficient data collection, analysis, and feedback gathering within your organization.

16. **Real-time Collaboration Features:**

- Leverage real-time collaboration features across Google Workspace applications to enhance teamwork and productivity.

17. **Sharing and Permissions:**

- Understand sharing settings and permissions to control access to your files and documents in Google Workspace.

18. **Version History and Revision Tracking:**

- Explore version history and revision tracking features to monitor changes and revert to previous versions when needed.

19. **Google Workspace Integration:**

- Learn how to integrate Google Workspace with other tools and applications for a seamless and interconnected digital environment.

20. **Best Practices for Team Productivity:**

- Implement best practices to foster team productivity, collaboration, and effective use of Google Workspace tools.

21. **Navigating Google Calendar:**

- Navigate through Google Calendar to effectively manage schedules, events, and appointments.

22. **Scheduling Meetings with Google Meet:**

- Master the art of scheduling and conducting virtual meetings using Google Meet for seamless communication.

23. **Calendar Sharing and Permissions:**

- Understand calendar sharing and permissions to coordinate schedules and enhance collaborative planning.

24. **Mobile Calendar and Meet Features:**

- Explore mobile features of Google Calendar and Meet for on-the-go access and efficient time management.

25. **Efficient Time Management Tips:**

- Implement time management tips and strategies to enhance personal and team productivity within Google Workspace.

26. **Introduction to Google Chat:**

- Familiarize yourself with Google Chat as a collaborative messaging platform for real-time communication.

27. **Collaborative Messaging in Spaces:**

- Explore collaborative messaging in Spaces, leveraging features for organized and efficient team communication.

28. **Real-time Communication Features:**

- Discover real-time communication features in Google Chat, enhancing the speed and efficiency of collaborative efforts.

29. **Integrating Chat and Email:**

- Integrate Google Chat and Gmail for a seamless communication experience, allowing users to transition effortlessly between chat and email.

30. **Best Practices for Effective Communication:**

- Implement best practices to enhance communication skills, fostering clear, concise, and collaborative interactions within Google Workspace.

31. **Google Workspace Security Features:**

- Explore the robust security features offered by Google Workspace to protect user data, maintain privacy, and ensure the integrity of collaborative tools.

32. **Privacy Settings and Controls:**

- Manage privacy settings and controls within Google Workspace to customize user experiences, control data access, and protect sensitive information.

33. **Data Backup and Recovery:**

- Implement data backup and recovery strategies within Google Workspace to safeguard critical information and ensure business continuity.

34. **Compliance and Governance:**

- Establish a comprehensive approach to compliance and governance within Google Workspace, aligning with legal, regulatory, and internal requirements.

35. **User Training and Awareness:**

- Empower users with training and awareness programs to enhance cybersecurity, promote best practices, and contribute to a secure digital environment.

In mastering Google Workspace, organizations and users can unlock the full potential of these collaborative tools, streamline workflows, and foster a culture of efficiency, security, and innovation. By continuously adapting to new features and staying informed about best practices, individuals and teams can navigate the evolving landscape of Google Workspace with confidence and competence.

www.ingramcontent.com/pod-product-compliance
Lightning Source LLC
LaVergne TN
LVHW022229200926
848481LV00006B/2186
9798223788010